Book of Anonymous Letters™
PART II

Amelia Anhalt and Kaitlyn Conmy

Dedicated To: All the letters never sent

You may be reading what was written to you

We first want to say how grateful we are that Part I was able to reach so many people.

When we created this project, we had no idea how many people would take such an interest.

One night, we were on the phone with each other talking about how cool it would be to write a book. We were bouncing ideas off of one another until we came up with one we both really liked.

"We should create a book full of anonymous letters from people all over the world!"

We stayed on the phone, and that night made a website where people could submit anonymous letters. We left instructions vague so that people could write whatever they wanted. That night, we posted a Tik Tok about it, not expecting much. When we woke up the next morning, it had gone viral. Within weeks, over 3 million people had seen our video, and so many of them wanted to write. So, a few weeks after that initial video went viral, we published Part I of *Book of Anonymous Letters*.

We are so thankful for the response that our first book received. We truly enjoy seeing what you guys have to say, whether it is through emailing, DMing us, or commenting on our posts. It means a lot to see how many people want to participate in this project. We started working on Part II right after we published Part I so that more letters could be shared with the world.

Regardless of whether your letter is in the book, thank you. Thank you for being along with us on this journey.

Thank you for writing a letter. And thank you for sharing your story.

TRIGGER WARNING
Many of these letters include stories about triggering topics, like sexual assault, abuse, rape, suicide, self-harm, depression, and eating disorders, among others. Please read with caution. We do not want these letters to traumatize anyone. When we launched the website, we did not realize that so many letters would be full of topics like these. However, we felt that we should include them because they expose lots of hardship and injustice in the world. People who have endured or are going through these things need to be heard.
We all need to be heard.

CONTENT WARNING
This book contains explicit language which may be offensive to some readers.
If the topics are triggering, or the language and/or content offensive, please do not read.

Resources
If you or anyone you know is struggling with any of the topics covered in these letters, including self-harm, suicidal thoughts, an eating disorder, depression, sexual assault, and domestic violence; please seek help. There are a lot of free resources out there and most states also have specialized free resources available, but here is a

To: My Town

I still love you, even though I've moved on to "bigger" things. Just because they're bigger, doesn't mean they're better. My favorite time of year is Christmas because it means I get to leave LA and come home to you. I finally get to sleep in my bed, walk to Alice's coffee shop, eat at my mom's diner, play paintball with my high school friends at the old shop, and listen to live music at the square. Last year, I made a big mistake and ruined my time with you. I brought Mathew home to meet my parents and show him around my favorite place. I don't know what I was thinking. That relationship was doomed to end soon, but I imagined it would at least survive the holidays. Instead of a happy Christmas with my gorgeous boyfriend, I was fighting in Alice's coffee shop and crying behind the counter of my mom's diner. I don't want to associate you with that winter, so this year, I am rediscovering all the reasons I used to love you.

To: Jake

You are a J name. I should have known from the start.

To: Time

My goal in life is to never take advantage of my time. I want to spend every minute basking in the world's beauty. I want to spend every hour laughing with my family and friends. I want to spend all of my days traveling and seeing different cultures. I want to spend all of my weeks in the present, watching the seasons change. I want to do all of this now because I don't have time to wait. So, to everyone reading this right now, now is the time. Pursue your dreams. Confess your love. Leave the situations that make you hurt. Write them a letter telling them how you truly feel. Do what you want to do, not what society expects of you. If it makes you feel alive, chase it. Live every day like it is your last. Because you only live once, so live it to the fullest. Because when the time finally catches up, you do not want to have any regrets. Right?

To: Al

I went back home for Thanksgiving, but I spent the whole time wishing you were there. I pictured you walking down the street and meeting my family and childhood friends. You would fit right in, and everyone would love you. I would love you. I do love you. I imagined your smile as I showed you what my city has to offer. Oh, you would love it so much. I dream of seeing your city as well. You say it's small, while mine is big. But if I am next to you, anything can be home. I imagine driving around your small town because that's all you say there is to do. You make everything entertaining, so I would not doubt it for a second if that was an offer. I was only gone for four days, but it felt like forever. Forever wondering what you were doing. Hoping you were having a good time. Hoping that you were hoping for me as well. Please tell me that you have imagined me in your hometown.

To: My Favorite Blonde Boy

I miss our summer fling. Meeting at a stupid party. Dancing in a sweaty room. Kissing in the backseat of your best friend's car. Laughing at dumb reality shows. Talking in the woods till dark. Getting drunk and hiding from my dad. I miss you. And I'm sorry. I ended things because I was too scared to be in an actual relationship. That's the truth, and again, I'm sorry. Now you won't talk to me. I should've known that it's too late. I have an unfortunate habit of ending things before they get too serious. Most of my friends have boyfriends, who they would kill to spend every second with. They don't understand why I'm so bad at commitment. I don't understand either. Just know that if it had to be anyone, it would be you.

To: The Person I Should Have Apologized To

I could go through all the excuses I gave everyone, but I can't lie to you for another second. You just know me too well. And you know that I should have apologized. Everything could be normal again if I wasn't so stubborn. I know it's way too late for us to be normal again, but an apology is better late than never. I'm sorry, Heather. You didn't deserve anything that I did to you. I'm sorry for lying about my past. I didn't want you to know about where I grew up or what my parents did for a living. It was embarrassing, and I wanted to be the perfect guy for you. I know I could've been honest or even a better liar, but I chose the worst option: pushing you away. You always tried to talk to me about things, but I snapped at you and told you I was busy. I'm sorry for making you think I didn't care. The reality is that you have made me finally face my past, and I am really thankful.

To: My Daycare Kiddos

This is funny because you guys are literally toddlers and preschoolers. But I cannot describe how much love you make me feel. From the hugs to the goofy things you say, there is never a day that goes by where I regret working at a daycare. Making friendships with you guys has saved me. You guys give me another reason to wake up in the morning. I feel so loved by all of you, and you hardly know me. You don't know about my life or my story, yet you chose to love me unconditionally. Watching you all grow up makes me miss being a kid and wish I still had that youth and happiness to play outside and make up imaginary games and have 0 worries. Working with all of you gives me the joy of my youth and memories as a child. I'm glad to teach and love all of you. You have saved me; every single one of you. I hope I impact you, and you can spread it as you grow older. I wish endless amounts of happiness for all of you in your life, and I will never forget you. Please don't forget me.

To: Nancy And Danny

You're both strangers to me, but I've been getting the Christmas cards you send to Etta for the past three years now, and I have no idea how to let you know she doesn't live here anymore. I'm not sure why she doesn't, or why you don't know, but it breaks my heart to think of her sitting, wondering why she doesn't receive cards from you guys anymore.

To: Those Who Are Afraid

Don't let the fear of what others think keep you from
doing something you love. Often we find ourselves holding
back because of a "what if." What if they laugh? What if I
fail? What if I can't do it? So what? What if it works out?
What if it's the best thing that ever happens to you, and
you'll never know because you're too scared to try? Never
let fear stop you.

To: The Random Lady That Stopped Me On The Bus

It was my birthday, and I was coming home from school. Nobody said happy birthday to me, not even my friends. I was going through so much in school and life and feeling like it was just not worth it to continue. But before I could get off the bus, you stopped me and told me that I was pretty. You do not know how much that means and how much it impacted me. I've thought about it since that day and will think about it for the rest of my life. I thank you for that.

To: Jessie

We talked in the line of the bar at my university. You only started a conversation with me because my friend won the Halloween trivia game. You recognized my costume and said it was cool. We talked about the character I dressed as while we waited to get drinks. It was a very small interaction, and I doubt you would remember. But I do, and I think about you sometimes. I don't enjoy the company of guys, not after the way one touched me. I've never dated or trusted guys. But you were different. I would love to be your friend, get to know you. I never got your full name, and I don't know your number. I tried to talk to some friends to see if I could at least connect back with you, but it's like you're a ghost. You're a cool guy, one which I want to be friends with. I think of you whenever I step into the bar on campus.

To: Flower Girl

It's been eight months since you died. You were only seventeen and didn't even make it a day after your birthday. And to answer what you last said to me, I do, in fact, love you too. You deserved all the flowers in the world.

To: The Summer Of 2017

I'm engaged but for some reason you and that summer always cross my mind.

To: B

I still have all the clothes you gave me and some I stole. I keep them in a bin at the top of my closet. I can't find myself getting rid of them. When I feel down, I put on your South Padre hoodie. I don't know what it is, but something about that hoodie makes me feel better. I still wear your chain every day, and I find myself texting you all the time, knowing you aren't mine anymore. I miss you. I miss how close we were. I miss my best friend. I miss everything, but I'm glad I still have some. I love you so much. Don't forget about me. Be good. Be safe. Stay out of trouble.

To: The Shadow Of Who I Once Was

It's funny how I never realized how much I had truly changed until I sat on a field and couldn't remember the last time I had smiled at the thought of what Christmas presents I would receive, that I no longer chased butterflies when they passed or smiled at strangers on the streets. How I no longer saw the good in someone and always assumed the worst, and how I no longer loved the worst parts of myself. It crept on me so slowly that I never realized the depth of my growth or decline. I wasn't angry at the world for what it had shown me as I grew older, but I was angry at humanity for giving a little girl with so much light and hope a piece of reality she could not attain. As I sat on that field and smiled at the sunset, I saw the shadow of who I once was. I also saw the reality of who I was becoming.

To: My First True Love

You know, I never thought we would ever come to an end. I always thought we would grow up, get married, have kids, watch them grow up, and grow old together. I guess everything good has to come to an end someday. I'm very thankful for everything you have done for me, taught me, and for being there during the hardest times in my life. I just have a few questions that never got answered. Yes, I know I'm hard to love, but you still loved me for me, and I don't get it. Did you want me, or did you just need me to pass some time? Was there ever someone else? Was there someone who could do things that I couldn't? Was there someone who you'd go to if I wasn't there? When you said you loved me, were you being honest, or was it a lie? I'll never know the answers to those questions. I'm always going to remember all of our fun memories, like the first time I ever met you, the first time I ever met your family, and cuddling on my best friend's couch when we got back from the lake. I remember when your best friend thought his window was down, and he tried to throw a bottle out, but the window was closed, and it chipped some of your windows. All we could do was laugh about it. I'm going to miss everything we had and did together, but our chapter ended, and now it's time to start a new one. You will forever be in my mind, and I hope I'll be in yours.

To: Papa

Every once in a while, I think of our happy moments. I think of our sunsets on the boat, late-night conversations, and the small moments when we were together. I still miss you. Just hoping you'd text me again asking when I was coming over next. I remember you getting sick and when you first had to shave your hair off. I remember you and me going on lots of ice cream or doughnut runs into town. I remember crying having to show you the dress I would wear to your funeral. I miss our birthday parties and when you would tell me I was your favorite person to share a birthday with. The worst was when you told me that you wanted to stop chemo. You said that you were sad about a lot, but the thing that hurt you the most was not being able to see me graduate, get married, and have my first kid. I want to tell you that I graduated last year. I got promoted, as I told you. I'm in college now. I have a boyfriend now, and he and you have similar personalities. I wish you could meet him. Y'all would talk about cars for hours. I wish I could hug you one more time. I wish I could have one more birthday with you. I wish I could have one last boat ride with you.

To: All The Broken Hearts And Souls

It's okay to be hurt. It's okay to be sad. It's okay to be angry or numb. But don't let those feelings conquer you. You're worth more. You're worth all the beautiful flowers, pretty rainbows, and dazzling smiles. Let the emotions manifest, and let them be felt. They must be felt to heal. Heal yourself, you beautiful soul. It's the only way to win and move on. Which is all you deserve and more.

To: Dillon

You were the problem. Everything you said was a lie.

To: My Best Friend

You saved me. You saved me when everyone else gave up on me. You were there for me during my worst times. Even when I let you down, you were still always there. You make me smile on the bad days. You somehow can find a way to stop my crying. You take the pain away. I will forever be grateful.

To: Frankie

When I first met you, I immediately knew you were my person. I've loved you every single day since we first met. It's not even a crush anymore. I'm in love with you a lot. From your hair to your eyes, your smile, your dimples, the way you smell, the way you feel, touch, talk. Your presence is enough to make me blush. Those soft smiles we give each other make my heart stop beating, and for a moment, and I imagine, you're mine.

To: My Mind

You have ruined me. You have ruined me in ways that I can not even begin to describe, in ways that have made me so exhausted. Is it so hard to ask for some silence? To ask for peace away from a mind that thinks too much? Away from thoughts so negative and degrading that any issues I may have were created by myself. There are times when I feel like I can't breathe when the airflow is too little, and the thoughts in my head are all-consuming, and I am just a victim of drowning. Drowning so deep into my head that I send myself into a spiral of anxiety and despair. But I can't blame anyone but myself. Yet I choose not to blame myself, and instead, I blame you: my mind. I think of you as a separate entity—something purposely trying to destroy me. In a way, you have succeeded. My bad days used to be far and few, but with you constantly in my head, with raging voices and intrusive thoughts, bad days have been more common. Sometimes I can barely get out of bed, barely feed myself, times where I become physically ill and want to vomit. You have ruined me and made me self-conscious. Am I too loud? Am I skinny enough? Am I pretty? How can I be prettier? Skinnier? Maybe I shouldn't eat, or I should work out, or I shouldn't talk so much. What if they hate me? I want it to stop, a million thoughts at a million miles an hour, so loud like the raging sea, and all I want is quiet. Quiet away from myself.

To: Linc

You've opened my eyes to a whole new meaning of living. You've brought out a new sense of adventure and light in me. You've taught me how to find beauty in everything. That the sky is painted different shades of color each sunrise and every sunset. How the ocean is peaceful and healing. That the mountains are waiting for us to explore them. How the sun kisses my skin, and the moon brightens my heart. That the trees dance with me and the stars guide me. Thank you for showing me how to love life.

To: Dad

I never got to tell you "I Love You" before you left us.
Those three words are really hard to say in a hospital
room surrounded by beeping machines. Those three
words are hard to mean when you have been told that the
person you love is no longer in the body that you have
been holding on to for days. Those three words have been
hard to say ever since that day. To be completely honest, I
think those three words will be hard to say for the rest of
my life because all I'll ever be able to think is that I
couldn't say them to you.

To: Caitlin

You used to say we were the "right people, wrong time," but it personally felt untrue to think that way. If we truly were the right people, there would never be a wrong time. We tell others we are focusing on ourselves, but I encounter things that remind me of you everywhere. It's hard not to, so I always let the beauty and unpredictability of life work its ways to keep your memory fully alive. And I would never challenge the universe for doing that; it's a blessing your memory continues to live on in the little things I find. Yes, the heartache and grief still linger, yet the reflection of your memory with the beauty of life overshadows those emotions. Sunflowers are your favorite; when the winter passes and spring arrives, I cannot wait to go to the sunflower field as I will see your memory bloom in all its glory. The second I met you, my heart was full of love. The second you left, my heart was overflowing. You aren't the same person I met that November 13th night, yet every version of yourself you have given me the privilege to see, I learned to fall in love with, especially the difficult versions throughout that period. It's so easy to miss love when it's gone and harder to miss it when it's there. I truly believe we were the wrong people at the right time, but maybe, hopefully, one day, in this lifetime or another, the stars will align, and every wrong will be turned right.

To: M

What was the point if you knew you were going to end up leaving in the end? You promised me so much more than you could ever give.

To: My Future Self

I hope one day you find the courage to let it all go. Let go of the trauma from your childhood with your brother. Let go of the constant letdowns that men have put you through. Let go of the worry and shame you feel for trying to help your brother while still having your own life. Let go of the pressure of trying to be the perfect child with good grades and a full-time job. Let go of the hurt you gained when you were assaulted. Let go of the blame you put on yourself for not being the person you have imagined in your head. Start enjoying life and all it has given you. I want you to find happiness in the silence and solitude in the loneliness. I want you to find joy in the people you surround yourself with and pride in the hard work you have already accomplished. I want you to be ambitious in your goals and be more spontaneous. I want you to accept that you can't change everyone to fit your guidelines. You can't beg people to want to love you and stay in your life if they aren't ready. You can't beat yourself up when someone shows you their true colors, and it lets you down. You must learn to be okay with yourself and your progress. Take a moment to breathe and smile about all that you have accomplished and all you will accomplish. And always remember to rise UP.

To: The Reader

Things I would've missed this year if I was successful in my attempt to not be here anymore: Finally figuring out how to make those five dollar gingerbread houses actually look good. Learning how to roller skate. Receiving a gorgeous bouquet sent to my house on Valentine's Day. Buying my favorite flannel ever. Baking my dog a peanut butter cookie for her 12th birthday. Understanding how to control my anxiety. Beating my eating disorder. Going to LBI for the first time in years and realizing how much I love it down there. Overcoming my driving anxiety and gaining my freedom back. Finding new friends that make me feel loved. Getting paid for my very first art commission. And last, but not least, finding him. To anyone who is or was struggling like I was, hang in there. This just might be the year where things will completely change for you in the best way. It did for me :) You got this.

To: E.G.

At least we're under the same sky, right?

To: Chloe

Thinking about the fact that I'm moving away from you soon is shattering my soul. You have been the best thing that has ever happened to me, and I hope you know how much I truly appreciate you. We only met a year ago, but it feels like we've been friends for many years. I love all our little inside jokes and how we obsess over the same small things. I love how we both enjoy the little things in life and feel safe talking about them with each other. You are my safe space, and nothing will ever change that. And being your best friend has made me realize that there are truly people out there that care about me. I never had a stable friendship, and many of my old ones have left me in an extremely dark chapter of my life, but you came right in and brightened it up. I love our trips to town and pointing out cool people on the street. I love how we both try not to panic when a cute girl comes up to talk to us. I love how open I can be with your family because they make me feel welcomed. I love how we have crushes on the same people and gush over them in the corridors (especially our art teacher). I love our Mario Kart competitions, guitar lessons, many trips to the cinema (and taking the same selfies every time), and many other things that make us such good friends. But most importantly, I love that you have always been there for me in my toughest times. You have always been someone I could rely on. Thank you for being the spark I needed to make me feel alive and more wanted than ever. Thank you for everything. Thank you for being my best friend.

To: Dad

I just wish you would say that you're proud of me.

To: Sadie

I love everything about you. I love your presence, humor, beautiful big eyes, and laughter. I can't stop thinking about you. I wish everyday to be loved by you. I wish everyday you'd love me the way I love you. I prayed for a miracle, that you would notice how much I love you. But... you never did. So here we are. Still just friends. I hope one day you find someone who loves you as much as I do. I hope you love them with everything you have. I hope you are just as obsessed with them as they are with you. I know it will never happen, but oh how I wish that person was me.

To: Depression

May we never meet again.

To: Whoever Needs To Hear

Because even though the world may be cruel, it's not cruel enough to separate two people who are made for each other.

To: Grace

I'm sorry I never noticed; the signs were there. I was a child, and so were you, but I can see the pain in your eyes, and I'm so sorry. You are the strongest person I know, and I will never leave your side. You are stronger than him and worth everything in the world. You are my sister, and I will always protect you.

To: The Boy From Freshman Year

I am so much more than my body. I am kind, caring, intelligent, and thoughtful. I wish you could see how I light up when I hear someone laugh or see a dog. I wish you knew my favorite color and my little brother's name. But all you see is my body. I could give you so much love. I want to give you so much love. I see how wonderful your mind is. I want to know you inside and out. But all you see is my body. All you want to know is my body.

To: My Room

Thank you for being the comfort I needed most when I was alone. Thank you for making me feel like I belong somewhere. Thank you for letting me decorate you with posters, paintings, poems, and whatever I could put up. You keep me safe when I feel I am not. Thank you for all the times I needed to be alone and still got the comfort of you. Thank you for being there for me when no one else could. I could never thank you enough for all the times I cried so hard I thought I couldn't pick myself back up. Or the times I laughed so hard I couldn't stop. I think about you when I am away and when I get back home just to be in my comfort. You have such warmth and love. I will always feel so secure in this room. This room has allowed me to make memories in the shortest time. I love the way you are so small. It's cozy and not too big. I don't need a lot of room anyways. I just can't help but think about when I have to move again. Thank you for everything and more you have done for me. My room has been my comfort and where my heart has belonged for the past three years. Thank you.

To: My Little Toe

I'm sorry you always hit the corner of my bed frame. Although you are a little crooked, you still fit in.

To: Pretty Hair

I did it. I finally dared to tell you how I feel, but everything shattered when you didn't feel the same. Nothing has changed between us and our lives because we still talk like it never happened. Nothing has changed in your view of me, but I'll always feel more than you ever did. I wish we had worked out. I wish it didn't end this way. For now, I'll still love you from afar. Keep on smiling, pretty boy.

To: Will

I want you to know that I think about you everyday.

To: My Mom

Mom, I miss you so much that it hurts every time I think about you. I know it's been four years, but it feels like only yesterday you were still with me. I miss the way you sang in the car so loud that you would miss the exits because you were distracted. I miss how you cared about animals so much that you would cry about the ones we couldn't save. I miss how you still looked strong on the sickest days. I miss how you would hug me like a baby, even though I was so much taller than you. I miss your traditional food and all the other plates you invented. I miss how you would wake me up every morning with kisses and a song. I miss everything about you, and it pains me to know that I'll never experience any of that again. I hope that wherever you are, you are happy and feel healthier than you ever felt because I know you were in pain. I love you so much, and I miss you with my whole heart.

To: The Man Who Hit Me

On my sixth birthday, a motorbike hit me. It was a stolen motorbike, and it didn't stop. I wonder if the driver thinks about me, the little girl he hit. I wonder if he lives life believing that little girl died that day. I like to think he has a little girl of his own and that he holds her hand every time she crosses the road.

To: You

It is getting worse every day. I see your smile, hear your laughter, and touch your skin. But there is no connection without commitment, so simply, you are not the one.

To: Him

I woke up this morning and didn't think about you for the first time since you left me. I'm supposed to be happy about it, right? I'm getting over you, but I'm not happy. I'm scared. Because once I think less about you and start forgetting you, I have to accept that it's really over. Completely over. Then I have to realize that I'm never going to fall asleep on your chest again, and I'll never be able to look into your warm brown eyes right in front of my face again. I don't know if I'm ready yet. And the moment I realized that today, I felt as sad as the first day.

To: Peg

It's been years, but I still think about the sparkle in your eyes that night. The way you looked at me and how everything else disappeared. I didn't believe love like that was real, but it is. It was. Remember that night we walked home hand in hand? I could feel how warm my cheeks were, but I wasn't sure if it was from the alcohol or having you by my side. Later that night, we slowly danced in your kitchen to Blue Christmas by Elvis, and you taught me how to waltz. All these years have passed, and I'm still trying to find you in everyone I meet. I worry that I will never find anyone else that will make me feel like that. Sure, I've had relationships since, but I have still never felt the warmth and love I felt with you. I hope one day our paths cross again. Until then, I always send you all my love, and I'll be cheering you on. You go get them, Peg. I'll be right here.

To: My Cats

I love you both equally, even though Max likes to cuddle me and Snowie only likes to lay down on my feet.

To: My School Friends

This will be our last Christmas together, and soon we'll go our separate ways. It's hard to believe how fast we're growing up. Six years ago, we were baking cookies for Santa, and now we scream breakup songs down Christmas Tree Lane. Life honestly feels like a dream right now. Everything seems to be moving so fast, and all I want is to hit pause. Nobody told me that growing up is so scary. Thinking about the future and imagining our lives without each other feels impossible. I will take as many photos and videos as I can to remember you when I'm older. You guys are my people. I grew up with you, and I'll never leave you behind. I hope you can say the same about me. I love you so much.

To: Him

I wish you understood and knew how I felt after everything happened. Yet, you will never know. It's been four months now, and I haven't even started to think about the possibility of getting over you. Every time I see a picture of you or scroll through my screenshots and see one of my messages, the feelings come rushing back. You will never see this, but I hope you know that I will never love anyone more than I loved you.

To: The Reader

I want you to know that you are beautiful. It doesn't matter if you have stretch marks, scars, acne, hair, etc. I want you to go to a mirror and stare at yourself. Look at yourself for a long time and look at all the beautiful features you have. Admire yourself. You are beautiful no matter what.

To: My First Love

When I tell anyone that I fell in love when I was ten, they don't believe me. I loved you with my whole heart. I was so proud of myself; that I could love someone so deeply. I wish we never got together because maybe I wouldn't be 22 and still dreaming of you every night.

To: Grandad

Words will never describe how much I miss you. The day we all sat together and found out you had cancer, we all thought you would be okay. The doctors said it wasn't bad and that they could do surgery to get rid of the cancer. Then we got told it was stage four, and they could do no surgery because it had spread too fast. I honestly remember feeling so empty and hopeless. I cried myself to sleep every single night. I couldn't even imagine a world without you. You and grandma came with us on holiday, and I remember noticing how much weight you had lost and how pale you looked. I felt so upset to see you that way. The last time I saw you, I couldn't believe my eyes. I had never seen you look so ill; I didn't even recognize you. It broke my heart. You still had a smile on your face when you knew things weren't looking good. When you passed away, I just couldn't believe it. I felt empty, lost, and sad. I was glad you were no longer in pain, but I just remember sitting at your funeral, crying my eyes out and going to do a speech holding the tears in. You were the best grandad I could have ever asked for. Nothing will ever be the same without you, and I can't wait to see you again someday. I miss your contagious laugh, how passionate and caring you were. You were my best friend. I miss you and love you.

To: Penny

I miss you more every day. I'm sorry that I couldn't say goodbye to you or be with you when you passed. I can't wait to tell you all the things that have happened to me recently. I hope one day I can tell you everything. We need to make up for the time I missed when I was gone. I appreciate the sky much more now. Thank you for helping me see the beauty in life; thank you for putting it there.

To: Leo

Thank you for treating me the way I've always wanted to be treated: like a princess. I hope we are forever like you pinky promised me. I love you more. <3

To: S

Why does loving you hurt so much?

To: Melody

You were my best friend and the best dog ever. I'm sorry I couldn't have given you a better life. It's been almost a year, and I still think about you. I'm sorry I was too busy with my phone or school to play with you. I'm sorry you weren't allowed to come inside. All I wanted was for you to fall asleep in bed with me. The day I left for a sleepover, I couldn't find you to say goodbye. A few days after I left, I begged to go home to see you, but Mum said no. She said that I had to stay with dad. Waking up the next day to hear you were gone was the worst thing that happened to me. I am so incredibly lonely without you. I never got to say goodbye that day. Goodbye Melo.

To: Everybody

A "hello" and a smile can light up so many strangers' days.

To: Amara

I think it's crazy how someone 4,412 miles away can make you feel more loved and safe than anyone has ever made you feel. Long-distance is hard, but I know one day we will both be able to live the dream we want with each other, as long as we both put in the effort.

To: All Of My Older Siblings That Are Gone

You're all gone, but not entirely. You're not dead. But you're gone. You don't talk to me anymore. You don't text me. You don't check in on me. So in my eyes, you're gone. I don't think you even realize how hurt I am by this. When I visited a while ago, you pretended as if nothing had happened. It was like we were all living together again. Every night I end up crying, hoping you will text me: "Hey, how are you doing?" But you don't. Because you all are gone. I haven't been able to tell you this but, I got accepted into a university and offered quite a bit of money. I'm probably going to end up going there, even though I was so set on going to my dream school. I haven't been able to tell you this, but I've stopped swimming almost completely. Mainly because I'm injured, but also because I've lost all my love and passion for it. I haven't been able to tell you this, but I've been struggling with food. I go through periods of not eating and then overeating. I haven't been able to tell you that I'm scared to leave home. I don't know what career I want or if I'm going to get worse away from home. I want to tell you all about the great things in my life and the things that are holding me back. I wish so badly that I could. But I can't, because you all are gone. You all left me. And I need to accept that.

To: All The People I Have Lost

Although you didn't make it till the end of my book, I will always remember the chapters you were in.

To: Amelia

I wish you'd look at me the way you do the stars. You look at them with innocence and admiration. You look at me like I'm merely a friend, which I'm grateful for, but I'd rather be so much more than that. I'd rather be your milky way.

To: The Man Who Assaulted Me

It has been almost four years. I still don't know who you are or why you chose to ruin a child's life. But you did. And even though my heart stops when someone rides past me on a bike, even though I flinch whenever someone's hand moves towards me, you didn't win. You didn't win, and you never fucking will. Because I am strong, and I am a survivor who you should be terrified to see when you walk down the street. You don't own me, my brain, or my body. I am still able to wear the clothes you touched. I can still walk past the car park you grabbed me from- right outside my school. I am still my own person because you will never have a hold on me. I am a survivor, and I always will be.

To: All The Characters Living Inside My Head

Thank you, you are my home. You are all the people I can never be, living in the worlds that I am not a part of. I hate that I am stuck in this world and will never have an epic love or be the main character. I will never be Aelin, or Feyre or Inej, I will never live in Terrassen or Velaris or Ketterdam. But when I read, you come to life in my head, and for a moment, I leave this world and enter a different one. You mean more to me than anyone and everything, and I know that while everything else is unknown, that friends and family will come and go throughout my life, you will always be there, waiting for me to come back. I spend so much time just waiting to go home, to be alone with my mind. You make me feel like myself. So thank you for letting me be part of something so great and magical, even if it's just temporary. You are my home.

ul Person Reading This

...n t know what you are going through, but you are
enough. Take care of yourself.

To: Sky

I love you more than you know, but I just can't say it yet. I appreciate everything you do for me: how you make me feel and how genuine you are. If anything ever happened to me, I would want you to know that I don't go a day without thinking about you. You make me so happy and proud. I work to be the best version of myself because of how amazing you are. The external happiness you bring me inspires me to find internal happiness. You make everything better. Thank you for being in my life and teaching me what it means to love and be loved.

To: Fin

Writing seems to be an integral part of us. When we first met, we went to a writing club together. Then we met again and wrote so many poems. I have a box full of folded letters and paper hearts from you. Now I'm writing you a letter, just to say I love you. That's all. I love you.

To: My Mother

I wish you would understand me more.

To: Harvey

You showed me life through your eyes, and I saw so much I didn't see before. You gave me a positive outlook on everything, taught me not to care, and helped me grow a thick skin. I don't hate you for the way it ended, but I smile because I'm happy it happened. I spent the best months of my life with you, and I hope that you look back on it and think the same. A bittersweet summer. I do miss you, but I'm happy you're living your life the way you want to live it- even if I'm not in it. I hope one day we can be friends and look back on all our memories. But for now, you must stay distant. I don't want to rely on you anymore for a happy state of mind. I must find that on my own now that you're gone.

To: The Lady At The Cafe

You have decreased the size of the chocolate chip muffins. You didn't think anyone would notice. I noticed. Either you bring back the big muffins, or you will lose the best muffin customer you have ever had.

To: Dev

Hey. It's been over eight months since we broke up. God. I didn't realize until now. When you left, I thought my world shattered. In fact, it did. I could not fathom my life without you as my boyfriend, and I did not know who I was. I sit here, eight months and four days later, with slightly more wisdom and knowledge. I know that I like to crochet and that my favorite sour keys are the red and orange ones. I know I love stargazing, chocolate, my cat, my sister, and spaghetti bolognese. I have accepted that I'm a bad vegetarian, but at least I'm trying. I know I love intensely and with my whole heart. I would not change that for the world. I picked myself back up after you uprooted my garden. I planted more seeds and filled my life with other hobbies, people, and experiences. I feel like myself again. You've come back into my life, and things are complicated. Old wounds are resurfacing; I'm learning how heartbreak does not leave you once they come back. Having them back will not patch your heart or magically make things better. Loving what broke you while you're broken? A recipe for hurt. Dev, you are my first true love. I know I will never stop loving you. You are home to me. I know your body like the back of my hand, and just touching you puts my soul at ease. Soon, it will be a year since we broke up. I don't want to be stuck on you. I want to move on and live my life. Yet, while I can imagine my life without you in it, I still don't want to. If only love was enough to make us happy.

To: Nanny

It's been two months. I still can't get over the fact that you are truly gone. I'm never going to see your beautiful face ever again. I'll never get one of your warm hugs that make me feel safer than ever. I'll never show you my uni room once it's fully decorated as we talked about. I won't ever introduce you to a boyfriend. You are never going to watch me get married or meet my kids. I don't think I've fully processed the fact that you are gone. Forever. I really wish I got to say a final goodbye, but I didn't. Holding your soft hand in that hospital room is the saddest I've felt, yet I felt so connected to you. You really were the best person alive, and I would do anything to say goodbye to you. I'm so sorry you've had to go through this, but I'm happy you are with Grampy now. Thank you for being by my side for the last 17 years. I don't think I'd be who I am today if I hadn't had you guiding me through my life - even at the hardest points. Our journey has ended sooner than we both expected, but it has been so inspiring. I hope that I can grow into your silhouette. I hope that I am making you proud and making the right decisions. Your funeral is in 25 days, and I'm unsure how to say goodbye, officially. All I can do is follow in your footsteps and make you proud. I will never love anyone more than you. Thank you for being the best nan a kid could ask for. I hope you and Grampy are now reunited and are having a blast. I love you to the moon and back, infinite times. I miss you.

To: Henna

I'm sorry I let myself love you. The way you bopped your head from side to side when a good song came on, how you stopped to appreciate colorful flowers, and how the sound of your laugh lit a room. The way the corners of your lips curled into a shy smile and your eyes grew bigger and brighter when you spoke about guitar or Harry Potter or your dog. I miss skipping school with you to grab bubblegum ice cream by the park and sitting by the lake - our lake - telling our most forbidden secrets. And those summer days, we lay on the grass after badminton, making the clouds into funny animals. Meeting you showed me a joy in life I had never seen before. All I had known was hurt and loneliness, and all of a sudden, it was just flutters of love and happiness. I chose to live. But as I crept into your life and fell in love with the world through your eyes, I failed to see certain darkness creep over you. I failed to notice your once sparkling eyes turn to stone. Those rosy cheeks lost their pink, and it seemed like you had become unfamiliar. Your love had melted and washed away. The ghost of you is a lingering shadow holding my heart down, all strings attached.

To: Love

I like being alone and not having to worry about anyone else. Yet I crave the feeling of being loved just as much as I love the feeling of being alone. I crave to be loved and cared for in a meaningful way. I crave to be someone's first choice. I want that connection to someone who understands my difficult self. I want to be loved despite my problems. I just want to be loved, even if it's not forever. I want to have that at least once.

To: Nico

You were my first love, and it's okay if you didn't feel the same way. I never really understood what love was before I met you; I fell in love with every little thing about you, from your love of music to your smile. I know we never really got a chance to discover what we could have had, but I'm so thankful for the time we spent together, even if it was only a short amount of time. The memories will stick with me forever, and if we do ever meet again, I won't let you go.

To: Andrew

Ask for my number already!!!!!

To: Ethan

How did we go from planning our wedding and writing love letters to not even talking? How can I pretend the boy I once deeply loved isn't mine anymore? I feel like no matter how much time passes, we will always have a part of each other in us. There will always be a little corner of my heart that will remember you. And even though you aren't mine anymore, I'm thankful I got to hold you while it lasted. I love you.

To: Jake Somethinghall

GIVE. THE. GOD. DAMN. SCARF. BACK.

To: Grief

Be still. Everything will be okay. Grief hits you in so many different stages of life. You can be grieving a friendship that isn't the way it once was anymore. You can be grieving a relationship that didn't work out. You can be grieving a loss of a loved one. You can be grieving your past selves. You can be grieving the city you once lived in and made so many memories in. It's a whirlwind of emotions that come and go. It is a part of life. Feel whatever sadness and grief you're feeling. It's okay. You're going to be okay.

To: The Girl On The Other Side Of The World

I'm glad we found each other again.

To: Society

I have learned from you this past year. I used to stare at all the people you would show me - with flat stomachs and round hips with perfectly symmetrical faces. Those people were beautiful, and I would look at myself in the mirror and think, "nobody would like this body" and "why am I not them?" It took a while for me to realize how the world truly is. Nobody is that perfect, and we all have our flaws. The reality is, we are all imperfect in our own perfect ways. I might not be skinny or have a pretty face, but I am still beautiful. And so is the person behind the camera I used to envy. And so is everyone else that was in my position. The only thing that's not beautiful is how we thought we had to look a certain way to be perfect.

To: My English Teacher

Thank you for reading the things I never had the courage
to say.

To: My Childhood Blanket

Where did you go? It would be really nice to see you again and have you at night, so I can fall into a deep sleep like I did when you were there. We went through so much together. Bloody noses, getting sucked up in a vacuum, and rips in your fabric from the family dog. But you were always there for me. Where did you go?

To: Everyone That Loves Music

https://youtu.be/dQw4w9WgXcQ

To: Auntie Rara

I miss you so much. I wish you were still here. Mum cries every time she sees, hears, or thinks about something that reminds her of you. She's falling apart, as everyone is. There's no more laughter around this family anymore because all of our best memories were with you. I had never seen uncle Dave crack until your funeral. He said the things you told me you never thought he would ever say to you. Marley and Louis wear your rings on a necklace to always have you with them. They miss you; we all do.

To: Anyone Struggling With Mental Illness

You are not your thoughts.

To: Future Me

Take time to focus on yourself for once, not on that one boy or the people that don't care about you. Focus on yourself! After all that you have been through in the last year, you deserve time for yourself.

To: My Sisters

I love you both so much. Thank you for always being there. No matter how far across the country we live from each other, you two are still in your childhood rooms, letting me bug you. I am so grateful I grew up with two amazing role models to look up to. Here's to many more memories we get to experience together.

To: The Boy Next Door

It's been days since I've sat next to you in your truck listening to Taylor Swift. It's been days since I've had a good conversation with you about our lives. It's been days since I've seen you smile or make jokes with your dad and cook with your mom. It's been way too long without you. I wish I could tell you how much I miss you. I am never really sure about a lot of things, but I am sure about you. Please know that I will wait for you.

To: Covid19

Sometimes I wish you never happened. I mean, you pretty much put my life on pause. But then I remember that if you never happened, I would be a completely different person. And I like me. So thank you for reminding me that everything happens for a reason.

To: Beau

You might decide to buy this book 10-20 years from now, and when you do, I hope you see this letter from your first love. Wherever you are, I will always have a space in my heart for you.

To: Parker

You took me on my first ever date, and it was a dream. We went stargazing and talked for hours. I've never told anyone this, but I have literally dreamed of that date. In the beginning, you were so sweet, with your words and good morning texts that never failed to put a smile on my face. I miss you - the person you were in the beginning. I'm starting to think that person doesn't exist anymore, or maybe they never did, and it was just a facade. I wish you weren't so confusing. I wish I could talk to you without having to decipher your words. I wish I could be certain that you wanted me for me and not for something else. I gave you another chance because I missed you, and I had hoped you would come back. And when you did, I was really glad. But what you don't know is that I am not the same person I was when we first met. I have grown so much in the last couple of months. I don't hate myself, and I know my worth, somewhat. Now I know that I deserve more than the bare minimum. I deserve someone who will move mountains for me. Someone who will love my whole being and who won't want me to change myself. I deserve those good morning texts. I deserve someone who you'll never be. Although nothing ever came of our time together, I don't regret it. Because the way I felt when I was with you was something I have never felt before. You made me feel so alive. You gave me butterflies, truly. But I haven't felt those flutters in a long while. And I know now that I have to move on. Goodbye.

To: EB

I'm tired of crying over you.

To: C.R.S.

I threw away your ashes. I had given away everything I received regarding your belongings, though memories of you can't be left so easily. I know now, at 28 years old, that nothing you did came from love. You psychologically and sexually abused me to the very end. Emptying your ashes into the garbage was the saddest moment of my life. Not for you. But for the little girl you stole. She begged me not to. She cried, screamed, and clawed at the back of my mind hoping to fight her way out within me. Hoping to salvage the last piece of herself that you had poisoned with your "love" in a tiny little jar. All of her was in that jar. But I need to grieve for her and finally lay her to rest in the grave you don't deserve.

To: Mooshoo My Baby On The Rainbow Bridge

The love I have for you will never die. Although you're not breathing the same air as mine, you're always on my mind. I see and hear you everywhere, but deep down, I know you aren't here anymore. I can never forget the way I hugged you as you took your last breath. They say you move on with your grief, and the faster you forget it, the better it is for you, but I don't think so. Rather than moving on and forgetting everything, I want to remember everything. Since every memory with you was worth it, even the painful ones. You would have turned eight years old in May, but instead, I'll be grieving your 1st anniversary. I miss you, baby boy. Please appear in my dream sometime soon.

To: Someone Worthy

I'm nearly 20, and the thought of not having someone kills me. I know I'm young, but part of me feels like time is running out. I feel like I'm missing the best years of my life because I'm so fixated on finding someone that cares for me. I guess time is everything we have and don't have. I look around, and all I see are couples in love. People that have found their other half. I don't think they will ever know what it's like to look up at the night sky and wish. I think the stars give me comfort. Because somewhere in this lonely, wide world, there is someone right for me. And perhaps, he too looks at the stars and wishes he was worthy.

To: My Pre-Shattered Heart

Dad isn't here anymore. He left. I only say this so that at two in the morning while you're waiting for him to get home, you won't wonder why you weren't enough for him to stay. You won't fall into a spiral of seeking validation from older men who just want to use you for your body. You won't think someone putting their hands on you and then buying you a gift afterward as an apology is love. If you stop caring now, you will learn to love yourself. You will learn that the only validation you need is yours, and you will learn that you are enough and no one is more important than yourself. I love you.

To: My Best Friend

I miss you every day. I know I'm lucky to see you even once a year, but it still doesn't feel like enough. You are so funny and inspiring and strong and beautiful. I always get scared that things will be awkward between us after spending so much time apart, but they never are. We always pick up right where we left off. The last time you visited, you told me about your suicide attempt. I immediately started crying. Not just because I wouldn't be able to bear your loss, but because the thought of your suffering is unbearable. You're such a special person, S. You need to know that I am here to support you through anything. I am only one Facetime call away. If you ever feel yourself sinking again, please know your best friend across the country is here if you need her. I love you so much.

To: Papa

It's been nine years since you died, and I'm starting to forget you. My mom tells me that you were my world. I would beg to stay longer at your house when I was younger because you had the funniest stories and cooked the best food. Every day that goes by, I forget more and more about you. It's a terrible feeling. I feel even worse for my mom, though. You were her best friend; did you know that? I don't even think she realizes how much she talks about you. From what mom tells me, you gave the best advice about everything. Boys, school, mean girls, and the future. She quotes you a lot and tells me how you inspired her to pursue her dreams. I miss you, but I'm thankful I have my mom to carry on your memory. I hope heaven is wonderful. Someday I will be there too, and we can meet again. I can't wait to hear all your stories that I was too young to understand when you were alive.

To: My First Grade Teacher

I had just lost my leg and was scared people were going to make fun of me. I didn't want to participate in the field day because I felt self-conscious. You told me to feel otherwise and to not let people stop me from achieving what I want. Thank you for carrying me to the finish line. I will never forget what you did for me. I hope I see you again someday.

To: Jilyssa

I sent our names to Mars. If we can't be together in this lifetime, I hope we can in the next. I love you always.

To: The Reader

You are absolutely capable of creating the life you can't stop thinking about. Stop living in your head. It's time to make things happen.

To: Brett

We met each other five years ago, and I've been in love with you ever since. Even though I've dated other people. Even though I've loved them. None of them are you. And there's nothing I can do about it. I wish you knew how much I think about you. I wish you knew exactly how I feel about you. One day I might have the courage to tell you. I know you feel the same. But you're scared too. It doesn't make sense how we got this bad luck. Why would the world make me fall in love with you just to be separated for the rest of our lives? We'll never be together with you over there and me over here. But I can't move there, and you can't move here. So what do we do? We were on the phone the other day, and you almost started this conversation. But you stopped yourself. I wish you didn't. Because then I would've told you everything, and maybe we'd be talking tonight. Maybe we'd be on the phone figuring out when we can see each other next. Maybe I'd decide to move there or you here. Maybe we'd be together. I guess we'll never know.

To: My Cousin Chase

I wish I got to see you one last time. I know why you did it.
I know you were unhappy, but I wish we got one last
picture, laugh, or hug from you. I miss you so much. I'm
just glad you're happy and finally free of the pain.

To: Society

Please be kind to others. Our time on this Earth is too short, and we can't waste a single second. The next time you see your parents, hug them tight. When you see your best friend, tell them how grateful you are for them. Even strangers deserve love. Being kind to someone can make their day and make you a whole lot happier. I've started complimenting strangers because watching them smile makes me so happy. I want to leave this world with no regrets, and I sure as hell know I would regret being an unhappy, rude person. I like to believe that the world will give you what you put out. If you're putting kindness and joy out into the world, the world will respond with kindness and joy. So, next time you see anyone, please be kind.

To: Mark

Thank you for helping me believe in love again, even though we didn't have a happy ending.

To: My Person

I realized over these months that I don't have any reason to want to be with you. But I still want to. Is that how you know you found your person? When you know that you can live without them, but you just don't want to? When you don't need the person, but instead you want them? I keep trying to forget you. People said that it would be easier with time, but no one taught me how to forget you when you are everywhere. You are in the couples that I see when I'm working. They laugh with each other as we did. You are in the music I play when it's just me and my headphones. You are in the places I visit, and I wish I could show you. You are everywhere I go. But at the same time, you are not. And that hurts.

To: Cloey

You were my best friend. You were there before I was born. I never lived a day without my favorite furry friend. You were there when my parents got divorced. You comforted me during my heartbreaks and made me happy on my best days. I loved giving you more treats than you were allowed, but you were old and deserved them. You were my little chubby black lab, and I loved you dearly. I never thought that I could live a day without you, and for the last nine months, it's been hard. Seeing you suffer from your tumor on your paw sucked. It did. I wish you never had to go through pain because maybe you would still be here. I miss seeing you when I come home from school. It was annoying when you barked at the back door, but I would do anything to hear your bark one last time. You were and will always be my best friend. I hope you are happy and pain-free. I love you so much, and I hope one day I will see you again.

To: Grandpa

Until we meet again, have fun in heaven playing cards and drinking with your friends. I can't wait to hug you, just know I love you deeply.

To: My Younger Self

Stop worrying about how you look, what you eat, how much you eat, or when you eat. Stop calling yourself ugly, and stop editing yourself to be skinnier in pictures so you can stomach the thought of being photographed. Stop skipping meals because you think it will help you lose weight. Stop cutting your skin just to feel something. Stop encouraging yourself to cut deeper because you like the blood. Stop staying up late thinking about how you'd do it and what you'd say in the note you left behind. Stop skipping class. Stop making excuses for him because he's never going to change. Leave him for good, and don't let him take any more of your heart and mind. Stop canceling plans with your friends.

Just so you know, you eventually stopped.

Now you're doing the best you ever have in school. Your grades have improved, and you're studying what you love. You have a great job that makes you happy, and you love doing it. You exercise regularly now and eat well. Your relationship with food is not perfect, but you're getting there. You finally left him and are beginning to repair the damage he caused. You made it through the darkest time and found your light. I'm so proud.

To: Anyone Who Relates

I don't really know how to describe it. Everything is different, and everything is gone. The music doesn't sound the same. Everyone got divorced or changed into a completely different person - not a good difference. Everyone hates everyone because of an opinion or a belief. But all I can think about is the Saturday mornings back when I woke up in my old neighborhood when I was younger. I'd play outside, and the music was good. Everyone seemed nicer, and I know for a fact that even though the world was chaotic, it still wasn't nearly as bad as today. Everyone was easy to figure out. I didn't worry about school. Life overall was just calm. Now I sit here (and I know I shouldn't), and I compare my new life to my old one. And I guess sometimes I just wish I could go back and tell everyone about everything that happened. The sad part isn't that the people and music have changed and hatred has spread. It's the part where we realize that calm life that we once knew is never coming back.

To: You

I used to say, "I love you to the moon and back" because the moon looked forever away. It was like no matter how many steps I took towards it, the moon and I still seemed endless miles apart. And that's what I tried to say. No matter how many steps we take, how many miles we walk, my love for you will be forever endless. I love you.

To: My Hairdresser

I try to come in and get my hair done as often as possible. You do such an amazing job and are one of my favorite people to talk to. I always marvel at how open you are with your clients and how easy it is to be open with you. I'm not even that open about my life with my family. You know about all my boy drama, girl drama, and personal struggles. I know all about your cheating ex, sick dog, and snooping aunt. Something about your presence is so comforting, and it makes me wish we could be friends outside of the salon - although there is something special about gossiping while getting your hair done. I'm going to think of something extra complicated for you to do with my hair next time so we can talk longer.

To: Grace

Sorry that I don't know what I did to hurt you.

To: My OCD

You made my life a living hell. Some people don't understand, but OCD is not just cleaning; it's also scary thoughts running through your head every second. It was so hard. You made me miss out on things because I was too busy crying and staying in bed. I was scared my head would tell me to do something over and over again. And after all those years, I survived you. So thank you. Thank you for making me realize how strong I am. To everyone out there with OCD, you are not alone. And it will get better, I promise.

To: The Girl On The Bus

I see you every morning when I get on the bus. You always have your headphones in. Maybe one day we could listen together?

To: The Little Quiet Girl Who Always Wanted To Be A Mom

You're going to see two beautiful pink lines. It's the moment you've waited your entire life for. It's everything you've ever wanted. You'll pick out names, buy little clothes and shoes, and wonder what they'll be like. You'll see their whole future unfolding before you. You will love them instantaneously with every fiber of your being. And then one day, something is off. You'll deny it and convince yourself everything is fine. But then comes this moment, where you can't deny it anymore. You will lose a part of your soul. And then it will happen again. And again. It will take you years, but you don't give up. You'll see specialists, have several surgeries, spend your entire life savings, and do multiple rounds of infertility treatment, and it will all be unsuccessful. But, you know what, little Mama? You're still going.

To: You

You're worth every single beautiful thing in this world. It's just up to you to start believing it.

To: The Girl In The Airport

Today, I found myself in the airport, sitting in the terminal waiting for my boarding announcement. You came and sat across from me. Brown eyes. Brown hair. Mascara rubbed under your eyes. You looked at me carefully. I looked back, but your eyes wandered. I went back to reading until I saw you look at me again. This time, it was softer, more somber. I caught your eyes in mine. I changed my eyes to gaze at your lips and then down to your feet. I know you saw my look, and I know you did the same, but I have to ask: Have you ever looked at a boy this way? Or is that just me falling in love with someone new every day?

To: Attention

I think I'm obsessed with you. I think I'm in love with you. And I hate it. I hate you and myself for it. Each time I lay in my bed, tears stream down my face, and I hold my phone in my hand, unsure if I should text a friend or not. Each time I can successfully go another day without eating, my phone is in my hand, unsure if I should call a friend or not. Each time I feel alone for no reason at all, my phone is in my hand, unsure if I should talk to a friend or not. I hate you. I hate that you rob me of my ability to reach out in every moment of struggle. I hate how my obsession with you made me feel invalidated in my suffering. I hate how my desire to have more of you fueled my every action. I hate you. I hate you. Because I thought talking about my suffering less would make it more valid. Because I thought if I reached out, the only reaction I would get was, "she's doing it for attention." And I was. I was doing it all for you. But maybe there's nothing wrong with that. Maybe I don't need a reason to feel sad. Maybe telling them how I feel, even though I have no "real" reason for feeling that way, is okay. Maybe telling them doesn't mean I'm suffering any less. Maybe it's time to stop seeing you as such a bad thing. I may always seek ways to validate my feelings. I may always feel like an impostor. But I hope we can learn to be friends. I hope to accept you as a part of who I am and learn that wanting you doesn't necessarily have to be bad. And I hope anyone reading this learns the same thing

I did: there is nothing wrong with seeking attention if that is what you are deprived of. And if you weren't deprived of it, you wouldn't be seeking it.

To: Hayden

Thank you for always being here for me. I couldn't have asked for a better friend. I hope your whole life is filled with joy and happiness. I hope you get a husky named Blade and live your dream pilot life. You would make a really good pilot. You deserve everything good coming your way. I hope you get everything you've always hoped for. I'm so proud of you. Thank you so much.

To: Shane

For the first time in so long, I feel love for someone. A very strong love. I don't have the courage to tell you face-to-face. From the first time I saw you years ago, I knew my feelings were strong. There is never a time where I am bored around you, or never a time where I feel sad around you. You have this infectious joy that is so wonderful. I want to know you so much more than what I've seen on the outside. I want to grow with you, help you when you're lost, and be someone you can cry to. You have no idea how much you mean to me. If I'm wrong about what message I have been getting from you, I guess I really am stupid and naive, and I'm sorry. But I can't just stand around and do nothing yet again. That is why I'm telling you. I want to find my bravery and courage again. I was so scared of everything, but I'm not afraid anymore. This is me, and I know what loving someone feels like. Anyways, now you know. I like you.

To: My Life

Thank you for everything you have given me. My friends, family, opportunities, and everything in between. I love you so incredibly much. I am so excited to see what else you bring me. Here's to the future. <3

To: J

The reason I always keep staying is because there is a part of me that thinks I can really change you.

To: Destin

I love you so much, but I could never be with you because of my family's beliefs. The months we've been talking have been the best months of my life, and I will never forget them. I'm hoping being friends works out until I get out of this toxic household, and I hope you stick around and wait for me.

To: Roxy

I don't know... this may be stupid. But you scare me. You scare me in the way you're so effortlessly pretty. And in the way, everybody obsesses over you. And in the way that I hardly know you, yet you've made me fall. Hard.

To: Past Me

The last time you wrote a letter, it was to your future self in hopes of achieving your dream. Well, I'm here to say that it happened. All the times you spent crying, feeling like a failure, feeling alone, wondering if any of this would be worth it turned out to be worth it. You have achieved your greatest dream and learned to love and trust yourself in the process. Great things come with patience and acceptance. You made it; Congratulations!

To: My Brother

It's been eight months since you passed away. I think of you every day and miss you dearly. I had a dream that you passed away three days before you did. I blame myself every day because I feel as if I could have told you about it and saved you. Although everyone says I couldn't have helped, I still have that in the back of my mind. I know you visit me in my dreams. I wish heaven had a phone or visiting hours. Let me tell you what you missed since you've been gone. I graduated high school and got a full ride into college out of state. I've met the best people down here, and they make me feel like I belong. Your daughter turned five (she looks a lot like me). I'm taking care of Nana for you, Bub. She's had the hardest time losing you. I know you're watching over me. Everything I do is for you. If you see Auntie up there, give her a hug for me. Every time I see a pretty sunset, it reminds me of you. I miss our fishing trips and our backyard camping. I got through my first semester of college! I know you're smiling and proud because all you wanted me to do was succeed through school. I love you so much, Bub, and miss you more than words can explain. Continue to watch over me and be my guardian angel! See you someday.

To: My Past Self

If you can't be yourself around them, why are you letting
them in your life?

To: My Pillow

I'm sorry for the blood, tears, eyeliner, and drool. I'm mostly sorry for the amount of time I spend on you. I'm sorry for not washing you. I'm sorry for hugging you so tightly when I needed it. I'm sorry for punching you to let out my feelings. I'm sorry for sitting on you. For throwing you across my room. I'm sorry for the paint and the hair you collected, and I'm sorry for using you until you weren't good anymore - until you felt uneven and bumpy. I'm sorry for letting bad people lie on you. I'm sorry. Thank you for being there through it all. You're the only one who was.

To: 2015

Being perfect is overrated.

To: Roger

I'll always keep the voicemail you sent me on August 9th :)

To: The One Who Left

You said you wouldn't. From the beginning, you said I deserved a family who could sit and enjoy time with each other at the dinner table. I never got it growing up, and you wanted to be the person who gave everything to me. Time and time again, you convinced me you wouldn't leave. But as time went on, it got harder to love me; it got harder to stay. I knew you were pulling away, and I broke myself trying to hold us together. You were my person, and you weren't supposed to leave. When you did, you took everyone I thought was here to stay: your family, our friends, your dog. Everything I thought I would get to have for the rest of my life, you took. I wish I could say I believed you when you said you wouldn't leave, but I didn't. I couldn't. I wanted to, but no one ever stays. You proved me right.

To: Pineapple On Pizza

I love you. Your creaminess with pop really inspires me to be a cool and crazy person. I don't know why I love the way you make me feel. I know some people hate you, but I truly love you. :)

To: Karens

Ma'am, you're too old for this.

To: Ethan

I still can't wrap my head around it all. It's been years. This is my second Christmas without you, and it still doesn't feel right. I still celebrate your birthday, and every year when March 16th inevitably comes back around, I light a candle and cry for a while. I know you can't read my texts anymore, but I hope you can see them from up there. I love you.

To: Karma

His name is Alex.

To: My First Love

It's hard for me to go a minute without talking to you. I struggle when you don't respond because I wish you feel half the way I feel for you. Part of me thinks you know, but another part of me knows you don't think about me in that way. I love you for who you are. I love you for everything you stand for. I love that you know who you are and are unapologetic about it. I get jealous when somebody else has your attention. I hate that you don't belong to me. You hugged me at a party, and I could've stayed in your arms forever. But the funny thing was that you didn't let go either. Maybe you were waiting for me to let go first, but I feel like you didn't want to let go. Whenever you talk to me, you grab my hand as if you want to be closer to me. That's one of my favorite things about you. Whenever you tell me something, you do it with energy and enthusiasm. Our hands touched, but instead of moving away, you slowly caressed my finger. I think you feel the same way about me as I do you, but neither will make a move in fear the other does not feel that way. But I want to yell from the rooftops my feelings for you. You deserve someone who loves you for you. I know I can be that for you, and I just wish you could see that. You don't believe in soulmates or love in the slightest, but I can show you what love is if you let me.

To: Anyone Who's Struggling To Find Their Happy

Someone asked me once, "how are you always so happy?"
I didn't have an answer for them, because there has never
been one reason I'm happy. There are many reasons. I
love my life. And I love living so much. I love the little
things in life, like going for a drive, watching the sunset,
and laughing with friends. Those things mean so much to
me. Life itself is so beautiful, and there are so many things
that make me happy. Even in the worst situations, I
believe there's ALWAYS something to be happy about.

To: Sebastian

You really helped me figure out who I am. I'm glad you broke my heart.

To: Brian

I loved you. And that scared you. So you left. Even now,
two and a half years later, I look for you in everything and
everyone. Forever and always, right?

To: My Favorite Person

I wish I could tell you this out loud, but words don't seem to come out when I try to. So, here it is. You're my favorite person. I want to spend all my time with you. I know you've been through a lot of hard stuff, and I am so proud of you for being who you are. I never told you, but I love you. I love you so much that it hurts when you don't respond to my texts. It hurts when you're not by my side when I wake up or fall asleep. I love you so much. I need you in my life. You make everything feel so calm. No matter what happens, you'll always have a special place in my heart. Your soul is my favorite thing in the world.

To: Me A Year Ago

I am finally clean. For two months! I know you worked so hard to get clean, and it finally paid off. I hope you're proud of me and know I am so proud of you for getting through it.

To: Lovers

Love is patient. Lust is selfish. Love and lust can look similar; please learn the difference. You will thank yourself in the end.

To: Early 2000's Chain Emails

I did it to myself: the painfully bad state of my love life. I didn't forward those chain emails that threatened seven years of bad luck in love, and I most certainly was not posting them to my Myspace page. I felt way too cool for that. The compounding interest in them must have been in the fine print because the years are starting to add up, and I'm still alone fighting the curse of the chain email in my love life in the form of mindless swipes on silly apps.

To: John

Your soul is made up of whatever is good in this world. Hot coffee on Sunday mornings. Sunshine peeking through translucent curtains. The smell of freshly mowed grass at the peak of summer. The first cold day of autumn. The beautiful sound of children's laughter. The pitter-patter of rain on a windowpane. The everlasting comfort of the moon. I only wish that our circumstances were different, and I had the chance to tell you this - to make this more than what it is. However, I will rest peacefully knowing that no matter what, I will always be able to call you my friend.

To: Mondays

People are too negative about you, but you're actually the best day of the week. I like to wake up on Mondays and pour myself a big cup of coffee. Then, I'll get dressed in something cute because it's the beginning of the week, and I have a ton of random motivation. And I think that's why I love Mondays. I love having a ton of random motivation. It's fun to get ready, do a mega intense workout, grind on my schoolwork, and start my week on a good note. Every Monday is another chance to have a great week. For me, it's almost like a challenge. How good can I make my Monday? How productive can I be? Don't have a bad attitude on a Monday because it might just ruin your week.

To: My Favorite Foster Kids

You guys made me realize how messed up the foster care system is. You made me realize why I want to work with kids. You gave me purpose. You're the highlight of my week. You provided me with a source to help change the foster care system. You're going to eventually have to teach me how to let go for good because one day, I'll wake up and get the news that you have been adopted. One day I'll look back and realize what an impact you made on me. Love you forever.

To: The Reader

I lost my right leg in a car crash on May 6, 2013. For eight years, that was the worst day of my life. I mourned the loss of my leg for eight years. I pitied myself for not being able to run in huge marathons or go on hikes with my family. I longed to take my dog on a walk around the block. And because I felt so sorry for myself, I was cold and bitter to everyone around me. I made them feel bad for having their legs, and slowly, people stopped giving me so much attention. I was mean and angry inside. It wasn't until a couple of months ago that I began to turn my life around. Something went off in my head, and I realized that I could have so much more than I was giving myself. Since August, I've been putting my life back together piece by piece. I go on dates now and cook meals for my kids. I got a promotion and started going to physical therapy. I made a complete lifestyle change, and I've never been happier. Real body positivity is accepting and embracing every part of your body. To anyone out there who has ever lost a body part, keep pushing. It gets better, I promise. You are so much more than your body.

To: Jay

I can't wait to marry you.

To: B

The last time I wrote an anonymous letter to you, I wrote about how much I missed you. After seeing my letter in the last book, I realized I didn't want to miss you anymore. So, I texted you. Since then, we have hung out four times. Everything feels better with you back in my life. I can't wait to see you again.

To: Dex

If you are reading this, because I know you love these books, meet me at our spot on December 3rd, 2022, at 8 PM. I'll be waiting.:)

To: Jade, Alex, And Malia

You guys are supposed to be my best friends, but I don't think you even notice me anymore. Every day I sink deeper and deeper into the most depressed state I've ever been in. I don't eat at lunch, go to soccer practice, or make conversation anymore. I used to go shopping with you guys on the weekends. But lately, I've been making excuses. School and work have been consuming me, and I can't stop stressing about the future. I don't like to be the center of attention, but I wish you guys would notice what's happening. Every day I get a little sadder and more detached from reality. I want to be happy again, but I feel so alone. If you ever read this, just know that I need you guys.

To: My Younger Self

It may seem as if everyone is accomplishing things before you, easily making friendships or finding their place in life. Keep running your own race through it all. You got this!

To: Reese

You pick me up every Friday night for some party or function, and it makes me feel like the most special girl in the world. You flatter me with the sweetest compliments and prettiest flowers. That special feeling never lasts, though. It leaves after your first drink. One drink leads to another, which leads to another, and then another. You eventually drop my hand and find another pretty brunette to flirt with. Every Friday night, I watch you laugh with, flirt with, and touch a girl who isn't me. And every Friday night, I find another scrawny blonde boy to go home with. I always leave the next morning feeling dirty and rotten. What hurts more than seeing you with other girls is knowing that I'm just as bad as you. I am sick of our torturous game. I want to be more to you than the girl you show up with.

To: The Flowers On My Nightstand

I love you because you remind me of him. Each of your red dusted petals represents his smile, and each stem symbolizes his love for me. I love looking at you before I go to sleep because it reminds me that I have a boy who cares about me. I am reminded that a boy is lying in bed, thinking about what bouquet to get his girlfriend next week. I think I'm the luckiest girlfriend alive. You are my favorite part of my room.

To: Survivors Who Never Got To Tell Anyone

I know nothing about you. I don't know your name, favorite color, or favorite spot. But I do know something. I know something happened to you, and it irked you every time you opened your eyes and even sometimes when you closed them. I know you never got closure or to hear someone say, "I believe you." It almost feels like a disease. It makes you stay in bed for hours and never want to speak to anyone again. It gives you chest pain and heartaches. The difference, however, is there is no cure. Spending hours on your phone trying to move on is no use. You will never get over it. However, you learn to live with it. You learn that it was not your fault. You learn you deserve nothing other than happiness. I, personally, haven't learned that yet, but I'm getting there, and you will too. Just because no one knows does not mean it didn't happen. You are valid, and I hope one day you find a cure.

To: Disneyland

I can't wait to see you again. I think you're my favorite place in the whole world. My parents have been taking me to visit you since I was a baby. I always have the most magical time, and I'm so excited for summer when I can come to eat Mickey Mouse beignets, ride Splash Mountain over and over, and run around New Orleans Square till closing. I like to ride Space Mountain first and then switch to the water rides in the afternoon. And ice cream during the firework show is always a must. I wish I could visit you more often, but you're so damn expensive!

To: The Man I'm Trying So Hard To Forget

If I had a penny for every time I've lied and said I was fine, I'd be able to buy the perfume I've been saving up for. Every time I lie, I feel sadder. I always think it's impossible to feel any worse, but then I lie, and somehow it is possible. The truth that I haven't been able to tell anyone is that the night of August 6th replays on a loop in my head all day. I can still feel your fingers gripping my arms and your hot breath in my ear. I would give anything to go back in time and make myself fight you off. I just felt so helpless. You took so much from me that night. You took my innocence, virginity, and happiness. I liked myself before that night. I liked my scattered freckles, the bump on my nose, and even my body. Now I'm insecure every time I step outside. I dress in baggy clothes and wear my mask just to hide my face. I feel like a victim: weak and small. It's one of the worst feelings ever.

To: The Lessons I've Learned

I wish I could have learned you differently, but you happened nonetheless. There are so many things I could have and should have done differently in my last relationship. However, I think I was supposed to fail. Because now I can use you to guide me in the future.

To: Frank

The way I love you has changed drastically. I loved you romantically and could not spare a day without you. I love you now in a way where I want to be there, cheering you on through your successes in the future. I feel pride when I look at you. I don't see myself as just your girlfriend. I see myself as your partner. We are like partners in crime, the way we build our futures separately but together. I love you in a way that I imagine husbands and wives should love each other, not boyfriends and girlfriends. I'm not infatuated with you; I'm in love with you. Thank you for coming back into my life. I love you, big-time nerd.

To: The Uninvited

Don't think you're not special because you're not invited to meaningless parties. I used to think I wasn't special, funny, or interesting because I stayed in on the weekends. I sat in my room watching Euphoria alone. I don't even know why I'm using the past tense; I still do this. You might feel lonely when you're at home on a Friday night, but you're certainly not alone. There is a lot more to life than high school parties. Hang in there, your time will come.

To: An Apology Letter For My Dearest Elise <3

I'm sorry. I'm sorry that you tried so desperately to fix everything and everyone in your life, but no one ever tried to help fix you. I'm sorry I never told anyone about anything. I'm sorry you tried to be someone you're not. You never deserved any of this. I wish you could see yourself as others see you and know what an amazing person you are. I know you think you are a burden and a bother, but you're not. There are not enough hours in the day for me to tell you how amazing of a person you are. I'm sorry you felt like a child and had no control over your life. I know he scared you, and after everything that happened, just know that you are so much stronger than he ever could be. You are the one person that has always been there for yourself. Don't be scared to speak your mind and yell at them. You're beautiful, powerful, intelligent, divine, and free. I'm sorry I was never truly there for you and ignored the signs. You were born to inspire and lead. Don't let anyone hold you down. Your greatest gift to the world is your ability to give others the same power and freedom you have. Know that you are loved and supported, even if you don't feel like it. You deserve the stars and planets, the first snowfall, and the first flowers in the spring. You feel like the sun and smell like the freshness of summer. You change the way people think, and you give hope. Every time you feel like time is slowing down, come back to this letter and remember that I am so proud of the person you are becoming, and I will always love you to the moon and back.

To: Dad

All I wanted was your presence. You decided that I wasn't important enough when I was just two years old. You are the reason why I shut people out, why I push everything away. You're the reason for the coldness on the outside that is supposed to cover the inner pain. I want to be good enough, but I didn't even get a chance to do that. Your last words hurt so deeply, but you were right: it's possible to grow up without a father. It just comes with a price, which you apparently weren't aware of at the time, or you wouldn't have done this to us.

To: The Academic Perfectionist

I understand why you feel the way you do. Why you doubt every little thing about yourself. Why nothing you do is perfect enough for your standards. Why you feel like you disappoint others when your academics aren't as perfect as you'd like. It's not easy to be an academic perfectionist. Trust me, because I know the feeling all too well. Despite getting good grades, doing all my work, and never missing a class, I still feel like it's not enough. I spend hours in the library instead of with friends, and I invest in study tools that I use way more than necessary. It all gets a little lonely sometimes. I feel like my friends don't have the same academic goals as me, so I often end up alone in a corner of the library for hours on end. I get it. It's no fun being an academic perfectionist. However, it's a part of me. If you're like me, I want to tell you that I'm proud of you. I don't hear that enough, and I assume you don't either. I am proud of you. It has been a difficult year, but you persevered. You did the best you could, and you never give yourself enough credit. I am so, so proud of you.

To: Fourth Of July

You're such an underrated holiday, but you're my favorite. I love waking up in the middle of summer, knowing I get to see a fireworks show later. I love putting on a blue bikini and jumping in the lake with friends. Nothing beats eating chips and burgers while tanning by the pool. Or blasting music through water-clogged speakers while eating a popsicle. Everything about you just screams "perfect summer day!" The Winter holidays are pretty awesome, but you're the only holiday that captures the meaning of summer.

To: Sean

Sean, There is no way you would ever read this. Even if somehow you did, you would never think it was me who wrote this to you. The past two months of knowing you have been some of the best in my entire life. I know you don't believe in fate, but I truly think we were meant to find each other. I love our late-night conversations and how often we talk about anything and everything. What I'm scared of is commitment. I'm scared that if whatever we have is on the verge of turning into anything more, I won't be able to fulfill your expectations. I'm not saying I like you yet; I'm still figuring out if I do. What I know is that your words and actions make me feel loved. I need that in my life at the moment. I hope we never drift apart and stay like this forever. Eventually, when the time is right, I'll be ready to take the next step with you.

To: My Uber Eats Driver

Hi, sorry for screeching "mmm chicken nuggies fill up my tummy" in a gremlin voice when you came to deliver my McDonald's. I could tell you were a bit frightened. My bad. Thanks for the food, though.

To: The Men Who Follow Me Home

I thought you only came out at night, but apparently, I was wrong. I learned my lesson after my 9:00 am spin class when one of you decided to follow me back to my apartment. I didn't go inside until you left, but I'm still scared from the experience. I feel like I can't go anywhere alone, which is scary because I live alone. I wonder if any of you know which room is mine. I really hope not. I prefer to be safe in my home. It sucks that I have to take such crazy measures to ensure my safety. I ask my mom to go grocery shopping with me, my friends to go to the gym with me, and my neighbor to walk me to my door at night. It's exhausting, but because of you, it's my life.

To: Thomas

I hope I always find you. In each lifetime. I hope that this universe lets our love live forever. I felt the sky shift that night in the field under the stars. Almost as if it all had finally locked into place. All of it. My whole life, I had looked for you in so many others. I collected fragments from them, pieces of your whole. How do I explain that it feels like I have always known you were coming? I anticipated you and felt you like the arrival of next year's spring in the middle of autumn. Thomas, I have always loved you. In every century, every second, every dimension. And I will always find you.

To: David

Sometimes I think about you. Not as much as I used to, of course, but there are always those moments when I catch myself wondering: where you are, what you're doing or how are you feeling? I'm at a point where I no longer feel pathetic when I wonder about you or feel anything when I think of you. You are your own special person, with your own complex life, and I've grown to respect that. I have grown. Even though you were never for me, you came into my life at the right time. And though I cried endless tears over the version of you that I'd created in my head, I thank you for it. You let me feel during a time I felt nothing, and you showed me how a person should treat other people. You taught me the sheer power of love, though never reciprocated. I thank you for it.

To: What Could Have Been

I used to want to be an actor. I don't know if that died because I was just simply a bad actor or if I looked into the mirror and realized I wouldn't make it past an audition room with a figure like mine. Then I wanted to be a fashion designer, though sometimes I think that came before the acting. That died because I was truly bad at sewing and anything related to fashion. Then in its wake, sparked a love of writing. I wrote, and I felt the contents of my brain leak out onto the paper better than I could ever paint them. I tried art occasionally throughout my life, but nothing ever worked like writing did for letting out my emotions. I think I reasoned it was because it was hard to make money in it. I wrote stories as a kid and showed them, and the moment I received criticism, I pulled back instantly. I clung to my art like it was a lifeline. I have struggled since to show my writing because it is my heart and the rawest portion of my brain. I wish I could have worked up the courage to show people, and maybe I'd sit amongst the covers of a bookstore. Then I figured since my concern was lack of money, I'd focus on a different passion. I always loved the medical field, so I switched my focus. I am a college student, now working towards this passion, but in my free hours, I still draw little sketches, write love poems to myself, and wonder where I went wrong. I still love the profession I am working towards, but the heart wants what it wants. My heart wants to act, write, and even draw. My heart wants to write epics and fantasies beyond comprehension. Yet, I sit in my college courses staring at PowerPoint slides of complicated biochemistry and find my brain drifting off to imagining myself as the lead in any movie or show. So to everyone reading this, follow your dreams. I think I finally will too.

Printed in Great Britain
by Amazon